GW00789068

MINI CLASSICS

HUSH-A-BYE, BABY

A Collection of
Prayers and Lullabies

ILLUSTRATED BY HELEN SMITH

∥ •PARRAGON• ∥

TITLES IN SERIES I AND II OF THE
MINI CLASSICS INCLUDE:

SERIES II

Beauty and the Beast
Brer Rabbit and Brer Fox
A Christmas Carol
The Hare and the Tortoise
How the Leopard Got His Spots
Jack and the Beanstalk
The Magic Carpet
The Night Before Christmas
Pinocchio
Rapunzel
Red Riding Hood
The Secret Garden
The Selfish Giant
Sinbad the Sailor
The Snow Queen
The Steadfast Tin Soldier
Thumbelina
The Walrus and the Carpenter
The Wind in the Willows I
The Wind in the Willows II

A PARRAGON BOOK

Published by
Parragon Books,
Unit 13–17, Avonbridge Trading Estate,
Atlantic Road, Avonmouth, Bristol BS11 9QD

Produced by
The Templar Company plc,
Pippbrook Mill, London Road, Dorking, Surrey RH4 1JE

Copyright © 1995 Parragon Book Service Limited

Designed by Mark Kingsley-Monks

Printed and bound in Great Britain

ISBN 1-85813-769-1

ROCK-A-BYE, BABY

Rock-a-bye, baby, thy cradle
is green;
Father's a nobleman,
mother's a queen;
And Betty's a lady, and wears
a gold ring;
And Johnny's a drummer,
and drums for the king.

HUSH-A-BYE, BABY

Hush-a-bye, baby, on the
tree top;
When the wind blows, the
cradle will rock;
When the bough breaks, the
cradle will fall;
Down will come baby, and
cradle, and all.

MATTHEW, MARK, LUKE, AND JOHN

Matthew, Mark, Luke,
and John,
Bless the bed that I lie on!
Four corners to my bed,
Four angels round
my head;
One to watch, one to pray,
And two to bear my
soul away!

NOW I WAKE

Now I wake and see
the light,
Thy love was with me
through the night;

To Thee I speak again
and pray
That Thou wilt lead me
all the day.
Amen.

ALL THINGS BRIGHT AND BEAUTIFUL

All things bright and
beautiful,
All creatures great
and small,
All things wise and
wonderful,
The Lord God made
them all.

13

Each little flower
that opens,
Each little bird that sings,
He made their
glowing colours,
He made their tiny wings.

The rich man in his castle,
The poor man at his gate,
God made them,
high or lowly,
And order'd their estate.

The purple-headed mountain,
The river running by,
The sunset and the morning
That brightens up the sky.

The cold wind in the winter,
The pleasant summer sun,
The ripe fruits
in the garden—
He made them every one.

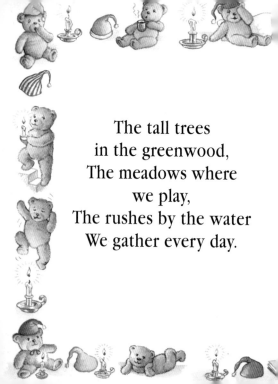

The tall trees
in the greenwood,
The meadows where
we play,
The rushes by the water
We gather every day.

He gave us eyes
to see them,
And lips that we might tell
How great is God Almighty
Who has made
all things well!

THANK YOU FOR THE WORLD SO SWEET

Thank you for the world
so sweet,
Thank you for the food
we eat,
Thank you for the birds
that sing,
Thank you, God,
for everything.

25

THE LAMB

Little lamb, who made thee?
Dost thou know who
made thee,
Gave thee life, and bade
thee feed
By the stream and o'er
the mead;
Gave thee clothing,
woolly, bright;
Gave thee such a tender voice,
Making all the vales rejoice?

Little lamb, who made thee?
Dost thou know who
made thee?
Little lamb, I'll tell thee;
Little lamb, I'll tell thee;

He is callèd by thy name,
For He calls Himself
a lamb;
He is meek and He is mild,
He became a little child.

I a child and thou a lamb,
We are called by His name.
Little lamb, God bless thee!
Little lamb, God bless thee!

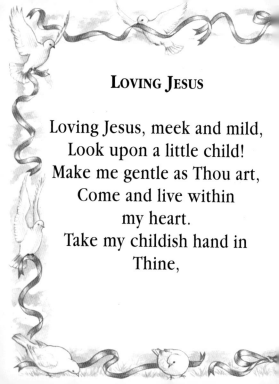

LOVING JESUS

Loving Jesus, meek and mild,
Look upon a little child!
Make me gentle as Thou art,
Come and live within
my heart.
Take my childish hand in
Thine,

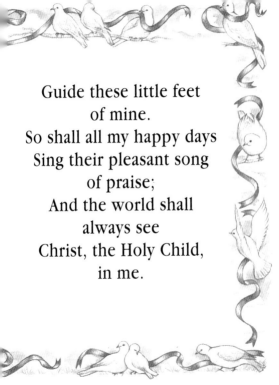

Guide these little feet
of mine.
So shall all my happy days
Sing their pleasant song
of praise;
And the world shall
always see
Christ, the Holy Child,
in me.

BEDTIME

Before the last good night
is said
And ere he tumbles
into bed,
A little child should have
a care
And not forget to say
a prayer

To God the Father
who, with love,
Looks down on children
from above
To guard them always,
night and day,
And guide their feet
upon the way.

NOW I LAY ME DOWN TO SLEEP

Now I lay me down to sleep,
I pray Thee, Lord,
my soul to keep;
Thy love stay with me
through the night
And wake me with the
morning light.
Amen

JESUS, TENDER SHEPHERD

Jesus, tender Shepherd,
hear me;
Bless thy little lamb tonight;
Through the darkness be
Thou near me,
Keep me safe till
morning light.

All this day thy hand
has led me,
And I thank thee
for thy care;
Thou has warmed me,
clothed and fed me;
Listen to my evening
prayer!

Let my sins be all forgiven;
Bless the friends
I love so well;
Take us all at last to heaven,
Happy there
with thee to dwell.

NOW THE DAY IS OVER

Now the day is over,
Night is drawing nigh,
Shadows of the evening
Steal across the sky;

Jesus, give the weary
Calm and sweet repose;
With thy tenderest blessing
May our eyelids close.

Grant to little children
Visions bright of thee;
Guard the sailors tossing
On the deep, blue sea.

Comfort every sufferer
Watching late in pain;
Those who plan some evil
From their sins restrain.

Through the long night
watches,
May thine angels spread
Their white wings above me,
Watching round my bed.

When the morning wakens,
Then may I arise
Pure, and fresh, and sinless
In thy holy eyes.
Amen

A Child's Prayer

Lord, teach a little child
to pray,
And oh, accept my prayer,
Thou canst hear all
the words I say,
For Thou art everywhere.
Amen

FATHER, WE THANK THEE

Father, we thank thee
for the night
And for the pleasant
morning light,
For rest and food
and loving care,
And all that makes
the world so fair.

Help us to do the things
we should,
To be to others
kind and good,
In all we do, in all we say,
To grow more loving
every day.

DEAR FATHER,
HEAR AND BLESS

Dear Father,
Hear and bless
Thy beasts
And singing birds:
And guard with tenderness
Small things
That have no words.

HEAVENLY FATHER, HEAR OUR PRAYER

Heavenly Father,
hear our prayer,
Keep us in Thy loving care.
Guard us through the
livelong day,

In our work and in our play.
Keep us pure and sweet
and true,
In everything we say and do.
Amen

HUSH, LITTLE BABY

Hush, little baby, don't say
a word,
Papa's gonna buy you
a mockingbird.
If that mockingbird
don't sing,
Papa's gonna buy you
a diamond ring.

If that diamond ring
turns to brass,
Pappa's gonna buy you
a looking glass.
If that looking glass
gets broke,
Pappa's gonna buy you
a billy goat.

If that billy goat don't pull,
Pappa's gonna buy you
a cart and bull.
If that cart and bull
turn over,
Pappa's gonna buy you
a dog named Rover.

If that dog named Rover
don't bark,
Pappa's gonna buy you
a horse and cart.
If that horse and cart
fall down,
You'll still be the sweetest
little baby in town.

CRADLE SONG

Sweet dreams, form a shade
O'er my lovely infant's head;
Sweet dreams of pleasant
streams
By happy, silent, moony
beams.

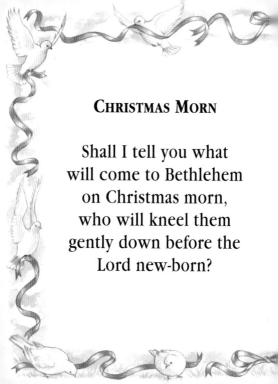

CHRISTMAS MORN

Shall I tell you what
will come to Bethlehem
on Christmas morn,
who will kneel them
gently down before the
Lord new-born?

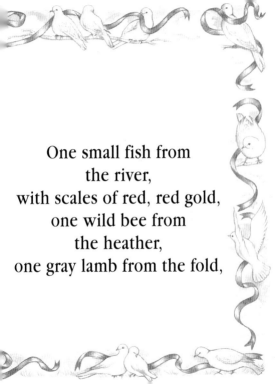

One small fish from
the river,
with scales of red, red gold,
one wild bee from
the heather,
one gray lamb from the fold,

one ox from the
high pasture,
one black bull from
the herd,
one goatling from the
far hills,
one white, white bird.
And many children —
God give them grace,
bearing tall candles to
light Mary's face.

WHAT CAN I GIVE HIM?

What can I give him,
Poor as I am?
If I were a shepherd
I would bring him a lamb;
If I were a wise man
I would do my part,
But what can I give him?
Give him my heart.

BE NEAR ME LORD JESUS

Be near me, Lord Jesus,
I ask You to stay
Close by me for ever,
and love me, I pray.
Bless all the dear children
in Thy tender care,
And fit us for Heaven,
to live with Thee there.

GOD BE IN MY HEAD

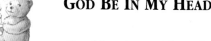

God be in my head,
And in my understanding;

God be in my eyes,
And in my looking;

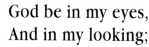

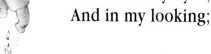

God be in my mouth,
And in my speaking;

God be in my heart,
And in my thinking;

God be at my end,
And at my departing.

HUSH! MY DEAR

Hush! my dear, lie still
and slumber,
Holy angels guard thy bed!
Heavenly blessings without
number
Gently falling on thy head.

Sleep, my babe;
thy food and raiment,
House and home,
thy friends provide;
All without thy care
or payment,
All thy wants are
well supplied.

May'st thou live
to know and fear Him
Trust and love Him
all thy days;
Then go dwell for ever
near Him
See His face, and sing
His praise!

GOD BLESS THE FIELD

God bless the field and bless
the furrow,
Stream and branch and
rabbit burrow,

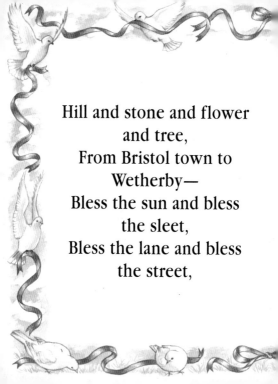

Hill and stone and flower
and tree,
From Bristol town to
Wetherby—
Bless the sun and bless
the sleet,
Bless the lane and bless
the street,

Bless the night and bless
the day,
From Somerset and
all the way
To the meadows of Cathay;

Bless the minnow, bless
the whale,
Bless the rainbow and
the hail,
Bless the nest and bless
the leaf,
Bless the righteous and
the thief,
Bless the wing and bless
the fin,
Bless the air I travel in,

Bless the mill and bless
the mouse
Bless the miller's
bricken house,
Bless the earth and bless
the sea,
GOD BLESS YOU AND
GOD BLESS ME.

LORD, TEACH ME

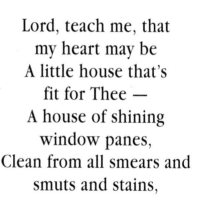

Lord, teach me, that
my heart may be
A little house that's
fit for Thee —
A house of shining
window panes,
Clean from all smears and
smuts and stains,

No blinds drawn darkly
down, to hide
The things that lie and
lurk inside,
And creep and mutter
in the night;
For honesty is free as light.

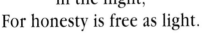

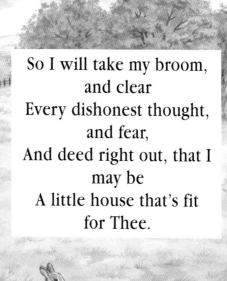

So I will take my broom,
and clear
Every dishonest thought,
and fear,
And deed right out, that I
may be
A little house that's fit
for Thee.

O FATHER OF GOODNESS

O Father of goodness,
We thank you each one
For happiness, healthiness.
Friendship and fun,
For good things we think of
And good things we do,
And all that is beautiful,
Loving and true.

COME TO THE WINDOW

Come to the window,
My baby with me,
And look at the stars
That shine on the sea!
There are two little stars
That play bo-peep,

With two little fish
Far down in the deep;
And two little frogs
Cry neap, neap, neap;
I see a dear baby
That should be asleep.